P9-CSA-547

Chameleons are lizards,
and lizards are reptiles,
like snakes, crocodiles, and tortoises.
There are about 4,000 kinds
of lizards altogether, including
around 120 different chameleons.
Just over half of all the types
of chameleons come from Madagascar,
a big island off the east coast of Africa.
Most of the others live
in mainland Africa.

DEC 1998

For my family M. J.   For Sam and Harry S. S.

Text copyright © 1997 by Martin Jenkins
Illustrations copyright © 1997 by Sue Shields

All rights reserved. First U.S. edition 1998

Library of Congress Cataloging-in-Publication Data
Jenkins, Martin.
Chameleons are cool / Martin Jenkins ;
illustrated by Sue Shields. — 1st U.S. ed.
Includes index.
Summary: Describes different kinds of chameleons,
examining their physical features, their behavior,
and their ability to change color.
ISBN 0-7636-0144-6
1. Chameleons—Juvenile literature. [1. Chameleons.]
I. Shields, Sue, date, ill. II. Title.
QL666.L23J46   1998   597'.95—DC21   97–4065

10 9 8 7 6 5 4 3 2 1

Printed in Singapore

This book was typeset in Calligraphic and Soupbone.
The pictures were done in ink and watercolor.

Candlewick Press
2067 Massachusetts Avenue
Cambridge, Massachusetts 02140

Chameleons Are Cool

Martin Jenkins

illustrated by
Sue Shields

CANDLEWICK PRESS
CAMBRIDGE, MASSACHUSETTS

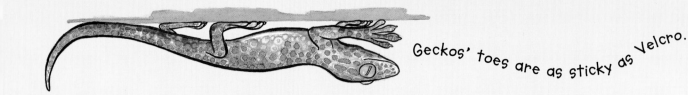

Geckos' toes are as sticky as Velcro.

Some lizards eat bananas—chameleons don't. Some lizards walk upside down on the ceiling—chameleons can't. There's even a lizard that glides from tree to tree— a chameleon certainly wouldn't do that!

The flying lizard glides on winglike flaps of skin.

Iguanas don't just eat bananas. They love all sorts of fruit.

But of all the different kinds of lizards,
I still think chameleons are the best.

Chameleons **are** cool.

It's not that they're all that big.
The biggest is only about
the size of a small cat.
It's called Oustalet's chameleon
and it lives in Madagascar.

Whatever their size, chameleons usually
get sick and die if kept as pets.
They're much better off left in the wild.

They can be really, really small, though. The smallest one could balance happily on your little finger. It's called the Dwarf Brookesia, and it lives in Madagascar, too.

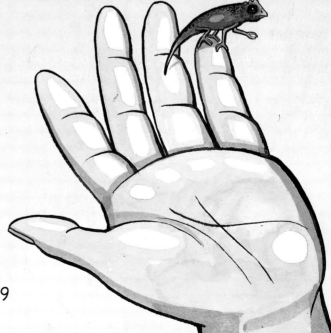

And I suppose you wouldn't exactly call
many of them beautiful. Their skin is
wrinkly and bumpy, and they've got
big bulgy eyes, while lots of them
have the most ridiculous ...

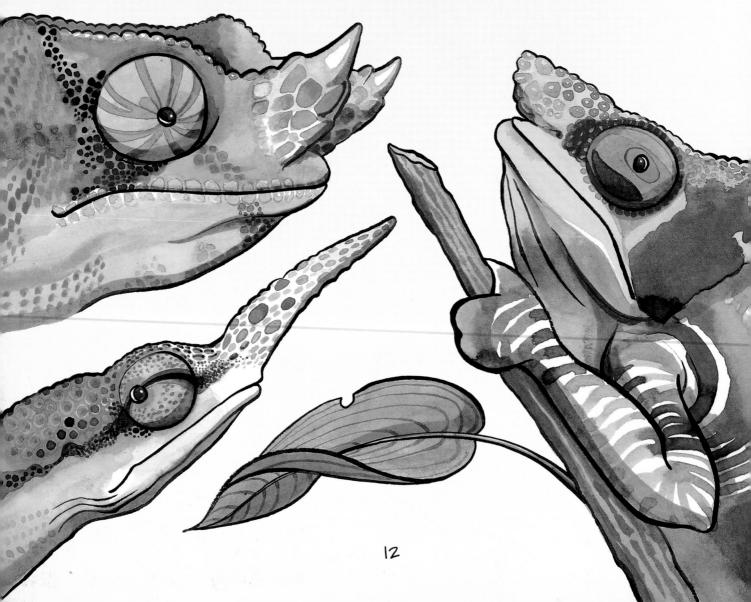

noses!

(I think it's their noses I like best.)

Their mouths are pretty odd, too.
They turn down at the corners,
which is why chameleons
always look grumpy.

Actually, they don't just look grumpy.
They **are** grumpy.
So if two chameleons bump into each other,
things can get pretty lively. There's lots
of puffing and hissing—and sometimes,
there's a real fight.

A chameleon will fight only with the same kind of chameleon as itself.

And that's when chameleons do what they're most famous for—they change color.

Lots of people think chameleons
change color to match
their surroundings.
They don't!

They change color when
they're angry, or when
they're too cold or
too hot, or when
they're sick.

And there are some sorts
of chameleons that hardly
change color at all.

As a rule, though, chameleons don't bump
into one another all that often. I suppose
it wouldn't be fair to call them lazy,
but they certainly don't move
any more than they have to.
And when they do,
it's almost always
incredibly
slowly.

A chameleon's feet are shaped
like pincers for holding on
to branches tightly.

Sometimes they stop completely
in midstep, as if they've
forgotten what they're
supposed to be doing.

But if you look closely,
you'll see that they're actually
carefully peering about.

Now, peering about is something chameleons
are rather good at. That's because
their eyes can move separately
from each other, unlike
our eyes, which always
move together.

Most of a chameleon's eye is covered in skin,
like the rest of its body.

There's a tiny peephole in the
middle that the chameleon sees through.

So while one eye is looking back over the chameleon's shoulder, the other one is scanning the branches ahead.

As soon as it spots something tasty, the chameleon fixes both eyes on its prey and begins to creep forward— even more slowly than usual. Then it opens its mouth just a crack, and . . .

23

Chameleons feed on all sorts of creepy crawlies.

The big ones also eat small birds, mice, and even other chameleons.

24

Out shoots this amazingly long tongue
with a sticky tip at the end, like a piece
of well-chewed chewing gum.

thwap!

Then the tongue flies back,
and there's a lot
of chomping
and chewing,
and perhaps
a few bits
of insect leg
fluttering to the ground.

Most lizards gulp their food down without chewing it, but chameleons grind everything up thoroughly!

And after that the chameleon just sits there for an hour or two, doing nothing very much at all, looking quite exhausted (and still grumpy) after all that hard work.

And there you have it.
How could you possibly
resist a pocket-sized,
bad-tempered, color-changing,
swivel-eyed, snail-paced,
long-tongued sharpshooter?

If chameleons aren't cool,
then I don't know what is!

Index

Look up the pages to find out about
all these chameleon things.
Don't forget to look at both kinds
of words—this kind and **this kind**.